Lanikai Bikepath 8K
July 11, 2010
Run for Fitness, Run for Fun!

Daniel's
Ocean Views

Inspirations of a Young Hiker

Compiled by his family
Joyce Cassen, Norman, and Sara Levey

ISBN-10: 1-56647-907-X
ISBN-13: 978-1-56647-907-3

Library of Congress Catalog Card Number: 2009929763

All photos by Daniel Levey unless noted
Design by Kyle Higa

First Printing September 2009

Mutual Publishing, LLC
1215 Center Street, Suite 210
Honolulu, Hawai'i 96816
Ph: 808-732-1709 / Fax: 808-734-4094
email: info@mutualpublishing.com
www.mutualpublishing.com

Printed in Korea

"A journey of a thousand miles begins with a single step."

– Lau-tzu

INTRODUCTION

This volume, *Daniel's Ocean Views,* marks the five year anniversary since Daniel's fall while hiking in the Nuuanu area. At age 19, he lived life to the fullest, and loved nature. A bench in his memory is dedicated at Sandy Beach, Oʻahu, Hawaiʻi, where he loved to watch the sunrise and play with the crabs digging their morning homes.

Daniel also loved inspirational quotes, and a number of these phrases were found in a time capsule that he put together a few years before his death. He would have wanted to share these, and therefore, we have combined them with his photos. His aim was to visit and photograph all four corners of Oʻahu: Kaʻena point, Kahuku point, the south shore, and Barber's point. He accomplished this.

This volume is a sequel to *Daniel's Views*, which includes mountains photographed on his final hike on July 21, 2003. His family has compiled this second inspirational book to coincide with the establishment of Daniel's bench at Sandy Beach, 2009.

We invite you, reader, to enjoy sitting at his bench whenever you pass by Sandy Beach. Additional photos taken are at http://geocities.com/hikefordaniel.

Respectfully,
Joyce, Norm, and Sara Levey

Sandy Beach, Joyce Cassen Levey, and bench dedicated to Daniel Levey. Photo by Thomas Ocasek
Background photo by Metod Lebar.

Photo by Metod Lebar.

"Either you run the day or
the day runs you."

– Jim Rohn

Panorama of Honolulu, O'ahu. Photo by Metod Lebar.

"Destiny is not a matter of change, but of choice. Not something to wish for, but to attain."

– William Jennings Bryan

Cable car track, Koko Crater, June 29, 2003. Photo by Daniel Levey.

"The men who try to do something and fail are infinitely better than those who try to do nothing and succeed."

– Lloyd Jones

Kamehame Ridge, Oʻahu. Photo by Daniel Levey.

"Experience is not what happens to you; it is what you do with what happens to you."

– Aldous Huxley

O'ahu coastline windward. Photo by Metod Lebar.

"One hundred percent of the shots you don't take don't go in."

– Wayne Gretzky

Puʻu Manamana ridge trail, Oʻahu. Photo by Metod Lebar.

"Kiss your life. Accept it, just as it is. Today. Now. So that those moments of happiness you're waiting for don't pass you by."

– Philip Bosman

Coconut Island, Windward O'ahu. Photo by Metod Lebar.

19

"Have nothing in your home that you do not know to be useful or believe to be beautiful."

– William Morris *(for Mom)*

'Ōhi'a lehua, O'ahu. Photo by Metod Lebar.

"What we see depends mainly on what we look for."

– John Lubbock

Hawaiian waterfalls. Photo by Metod Lebar.

"Vision without action is a daydream. Action without vision is a nightmare."

– Japanese proverb

Pali Summit, O'ahu. Photo by Metod Lebar.

"Now is the time. Needs are great but your possiblilities are greater."

– Bill Blackman

Koʻolau Summit Trail, Oʻahu. Photo by Metod Lebar.

"The foolish man seeks
happiness in the distance,
the wise grows it under
his feet."

– James Oppenheim

Trail flowers. Photo by Metod Lebar.

"Better to light one small candle than to curse the darkness."

– Chinese proverb

Sunset, Sandy Beach, Oʻahu. Photo by Daniel Levey.

"I do not think much of a man who does not know more today than he did yesterday."

– Abraham Lincoln

Looking Windward, Oʻahu. Photo by Metod Lebar.

"The true measure of a man is how he treats someone who can do him absolutely no good."

– Ann Landers

Sandy Beach, Oʻahu South Shore. Photo by Daniel Levey.

"We are not human beings on a spiritual journey. We are spiritual beings on a human journey."

– Steven Covey

"Crab Beach" at Sandy Beach, Oʻahu. Photo by Daniel Levey.

"How wonderful it is that we can start doing good at this very moment."

– Anne Frank

Kāneʻohe Bay, Windward Oʻahu. Photo by Metod Lebar.

"Man cannot discover new oceans unless he has the courage to lose sight of the shore."

– Andre Gide

Windward view, Kamehame Ridge. Photo by Joyce Cassen Levey.

"The best way out is always through."

– Robert Frost

View from Lanipo Trail, Kahala. Photo by Metod Lebar.

"Life can only be understood backwards, but it must be lived forwards."

– Søren Kierkegaard

Puʻu Manamana Ridge trail, Windward Oʻahu. Photo by Metod Lebar.

"The unexamined life is not worth living."

– Socrates

Koko Crater. Photo by Daniel Levey.

"Know thyself."

– Socrates

Fishponds, Mokoli'i. Photo by Metod Lebar.

"There are two ways to live your life. One is as though nothing is a miracle. The other is as though everything is a miracle."

– Albert Einstein

Waiʻanae Mountain Range. Photo by Metod Lebar.

"The butterfly counts not
months but moments,
and has time enough."

– Rabindranath Tagore

Koʻolau Summit Trail, Oʻahu. Photo by Metod Lebar.

"Do not go where the path may lead, go instead where there is no path and leave a trail."

– Ralph Waldo Emerson

Kamehame Ridge, Hang Glider's Platform. Photo by Joyce Cassen Levey.

"Exit light,
Enter night,
Take my hand,
Off to never never land"

– "Enter Sandman," Metallica

Nuʻuanu Lookout (Reservoir 4, adjacent to Pali Hwy), Oʻahu. Photo by Metod Lebar.

"Climb the mountains and get their good tidings. Nature's peace will flow into you as sunshine flows into trees. The winds will blow their own freshness into you, and the storms their energy, while cares will drop off like autumn leaves."

– John Muir

Sandy Beach, O'ahu. Photo by Daniel Levey.

"You need special shoes for hiking - and a bit of a special soul as well."

– Emme Woodhull-Bäche

Hikers on Puʻu Manamana trail, Oʻahu. Photo by Metod Lebar.

"In all things of nature
there is something of the
marvelous."

– Aristotle

Kahana Bay, Oʻahu. Photo by Metod Lebar.

63

Daniel's List of 100 things to do

1. Visit the Amazon
2. Visit the Gettysburg Battlefield
3. Visit Pompeii, Italy
4. Visit Ibiza, Spain
5. Visit Yosemite National Park
6. Visit Area 51
7. Visit meteor crater (done)
8. Visit the Hollywood sign
9. Swim with dolphins (done)
10. Go to Minsk, Belarus
11. See Saint Basil's Cathedral
12. See Lenin's Mausoleum
13. Watch the Kentucky Derby
14. Visit Alcatraz

15. Float in the Dead Sea (done)
16. Go to the Galapagos Islands
17. Go to the Goldeneye retreat in Jamaica
18. Play golf at St. Andrews in Scotland
19. Visit the Blue Lagoon in Reykjavik, Iceland
20. Visit the Martin Luther King Jr. Memorial in Atlanta, Georgia
21. See Barnum and Bailey Circus
22. Visit Stonehenge
23. Visit Hiroshima, Japan
24. Run a marathon (done)
25. Cage dive with great white sharks
26. Visit the Acropolis
27. Visit the Vatican
28. Visit San Marino
29. Visit Monaco

30. Bicycle across the U.S.
31. Eat fugu
32. Visit Vietnam War memorial
33. Visit Graceland
34. Go whitewater rafting (done)
35. Eat a meal good enough to be your last (at Chadwick Restaurant in Beverly Hills, CA)
36. La Tomatina festival in Spain
37. Visit Grand Canyon (done)
38. Watch a performance of Shakespeare's Hamlet play
39. Ride a gondola in Venice, Italy
40. Bungee jump
41. Skydive
42. Kiss the Blarney stone
43. Attend a fashion show in Milan, Italy

44. Visit Hershey's Chocolate World in Pennsylvania
45. Run with the bulls in Pamplona, Spain
46. Take a San Francisco trolley ride (done)
47. Chase a tornado
48. Visit the Holocaust Museum
49. Visit Great Wall of China
50. Visit the Louvre
51. Visit the Smithsonian Museums
52. Visit Mount Kilimanjaro
53. Visit Mount Everest
54. Visit Mount Fuji (done)
55. Visit the Ganges River
56. Visit the Nile River
57. Visit Machu Picchu
58. Visit Taj Mahal

59. Visit the Great Pyramid of Giza
60. Visit Hoover Dam (done)
61. Go through the Panama Canal
62. Visit the Petronas Twin Towers in Kuala Lumpur, Malaysia
63. Take a ride in the Chunnel
64. See the Statue of Liberty
65. See the sunrise from Haleakala
66. Take a steamboat down the Mississippi River
67. Watch the changing of the guard at Buckingham Palace
68. See Michelangelo's David in Florence, Italy
69. Stay in Lizzy Borden's house in Fall River, Massachusetts
70. Go to the San Juan Islands in Washington to see orcas

71. Visit the Angkor Wat in Cambodia
72. Take a trip on the Orient Express
73. Visit Burning Man festival
74. See the Northern lights
75. Visit the New York Public Library
76. Experience a nuclear submarine emergency surface
77. New Year's in Times Square
78. Attend Mardi Gras
79. Attend Carnival
80. Attend the vegetarian festival in Singapore
81. Attend a NASCAR race
82. Visit the Keck Observatory at the top of Mauna Kea
83. Visit the blue grotto in Capri
84. Celebrate the Day of the Dead in Mexico

85. Witness a volcanic eruption (done)
86. Go on an African safari
87. Take a ride in a Ferrari
88. See the Crazy Horse memorial
89. Visit Paris
90. Watch a space shuttle launch
91. Visit Xian
92. Visit T'ai Shan
93. Visit Chaco Canyon, New Mexico
94. Visit Chichen Itza
95. Visit Masada (done)
96. Visit the Western Wall in Jerusalem (done)
97. Visit Las Vegas (done)
98. Visit Knossos
99. See the midnight sun (done)
100. Stay at the Ice Hotel in Sweden

Reflections/Notes

_____

_____

_____

_____

_____

_____

_____

_____

_____

_____